MIND VS. MUSCLE

THE PSYCHOLOGY OF SPORTS

BASEBALL

CATHLEEN SMALL

Gareth Stevens
PUBLISHING

Please visit our website, **www.garethstevens.com**.
For a free color catalog of all our high-quality books,
call toll free 1-800-542-2595 or fax 1-877-542-2596.

Cataloging-in-Publication Data

Names: Small, Cathleen.
Title: Baseball / Cathleen Small.
Description: New York : Gareth Stevens Publishing, 2019. | Series: Mind vs muscle: the
psychology of sports | Includes glossary and index.
Identifiers: LCCN ISBN 9781538225370 (pbk.) | ISBN 9781538225448 (library bound)
Subjects: LCSH: Baseball--Juvenile literature.
Classification: LCC GV867.5 S63 2019 | DDC 796.357--dc23

First Edition

Published in 2019 by
Gareth Stevens Publishing
111 East 14th Street, Suite 349
New York, NY 10003

Produced for Gareth Stevens by Calcium Creative Ltd
Editors: Sarah Eason and Jennifer Sanderson
Designers: Paul Myerscough and Simon Borrough
Picture researcher: Rachel Blount

Picture credits: Cover: Shutterstock: Photo Works; Inside: Shutterstock: Akihirohatako:
p. 22; Aspen Photo: pp. 25, 29, 36, 37, 38; Brocreative: p. 32; Ben Carlson: p. 13; Crevis:
p. 7; DarioZg: pp. 16, 30; Dizain: p. 4; Elvisvaughn: p. 11b; Keeton Gale: p. 45; Will Hughes:
pp. 1, 33; Richard Paul Kane: p. 24; Andrew F. Kazmiersk: p. 8; Mike Liu: p. 35;
Mr. Chuckles: p. 18; MTaira: p. 27; Nagel Photography: p. 34; Andrei Orlov: p. 5; Photo
Works: p. 20; Razorbeam: p. 28; Lauren Simmons: p. 17; Sirtravelalot: pp. 23, 39, 40, 41, 43;
Tammykayphoto: p. 21; Jeff Thrower: p. 15; Tony-Gibson: p. 31; Suzanne Tucker: p. 42;
Vector FX: p. 26; Wavebreakmedia: p. 14; Andrey Yurlov: p. 9; Wikimedia Commons:
Charles M. Conlon: p. 6; Harris & Ewing: pp. 10-11; Bowman Gum: p. 19; Louis Van Oeyen:
p. 44; Sam Smith: p. 12.

Printed in the United States of America

CPSIA compliance information: Batch #CS18GS:
For further information contact Gareth Stevens, New York, New York at 1-800-542-2595.

CONTENTS

CHAPTER 1

THE PSYCHOLOGY OF Sports

In any sport, **athleticism** may count for a lot, but **psychology** is just as, if not more, important. Players have to anticipate the strengths of their opponents and use that information to plan their own strategies. They also have to assess their opponents' weaknesses and use that knowledge to form their plan of attack. If an opponent has a weak spot—and everyone has a weak spot—players can use psychology to determine how best to exploit that weakness.

Psychology is used to help people in many areas. In general, psychology helps people gain a better understanding of themselves and how they react to situations. It is not uncommon for people to work with psychologists to help them manage stress or anxiety, or learn how to better deal with challenges in their everyday lives.

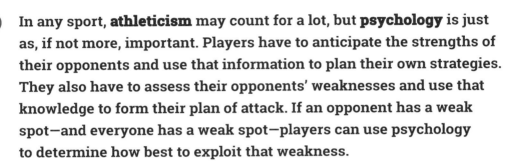

Many factors go into living a healthy, happy life—one of which is an understanding of how we react to situations.

The same is true in the world of sports. Psychology can help athletes perform better and improve on any weaknesses they may have. It can also teach them to focus and relax, which is crucial for them to perform at the top of their game.

WHAT IS SPORTS PSYCHOLOGY?

Some might think that sports psychology is a new field, but that is far from true. In the late 1800s, psychologist Norman Triplett studied the psychology behind cycling. In 1925, the first U.S. sports psychology laboratory was founded at the University of Illinois. Around the same time, psychologists at Stanford University in California were working on experiments related to the psychology of football.

Sports psychology can improve a player's game at any age. By learning to manage their thoughts while young, a player will be well-prepared for their future career.

Early psychology studies were done in a variety of sports, and baseball was one of them. In fact, sports psychologists used legendary hitter Babe Ruth as the subject of an early experiment. In it, psychologists combined principles of **neuroscience** with psychology to help them understand how Ruth became such a powerful player.

ALL IN THE MIND

Babe Ruth: Removing Distractions

Babe Ruth had a phenomenal baseball season in 1920, which he ended with 172 hits, a record-breaking 54 home runs, and 137 runs batted in. Psychologists wanted to understand what made him such an amazing hitter, so in 1921, they ran several tests on him at Columbia University in New York. The tests measured his **coordination**, memory, vision, reaction time, and intelligence, among other things.

From the tests, they learned that Ruth's eyes processed about 12 percent faster than the average person's, and his nerves were steadier than 499 out of 500 people. His intelligence measured at 10 percent above average. In attention and quickness of **perception**, he was found to be 1.5 times above the average person.

Ruth's coaches and team manager had to decide what to do with this information. Looking back at past seasons, they realized that Ruth had most likely done so well in the 1920 season because he had not been distracted by pitching and studying other batters. Prior to 1920, Ruth had been a pitcher. But by 1920, he had switched to batting. Once the distraction of pitching was removed, Babe Ruth's batting record skyrocketed.

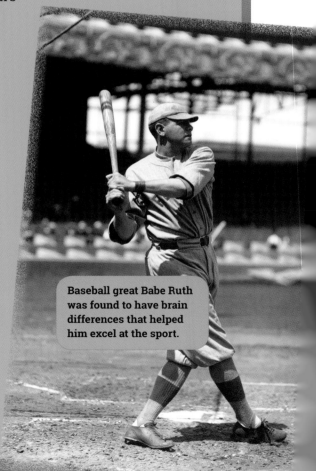

Baseball great Babe Ruth was found to have brain differences that helped him excel at the sport.

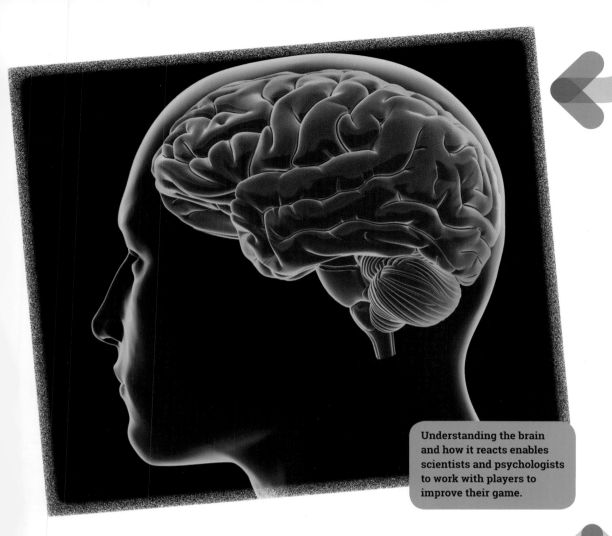

Understanding the brain and how it reacts enables scientists and psychologists to work with players to improve their game.

COMBINING NEUROSCIENCE AND PSYCHOLOGY

In the years since the early studies on Babe Ruth, sports psychologists have continued to combine neuroscience with psychology to help athletes excel. For example, a research group out of the United Kingdom called Applied Cognitive Neuroscience has made sports and the brain a large part of its focus. Applied Cognitive Neuroscience is dedicated to combining the fields of neuroscience and psychology to help athletes better their performance on the field. Countless articles have also been published in scientific journals about the fields of neuroscience and psychology in relation to sports and athletes. It is an ever-growing field of study.

As well as considering how neuroscience can work with psychology in athletics, sports psychologists also work on a more practical level. They teach teams and individual athletes strategies, such as **visualization** and **goal setting**, that can help them improve their performance.

Overall, sports psychology looks at how participating in sports affects an athlete's **mental state** and how an athlete's mental state can affect their performance. Sports psychologists work with individuals, but they also work with the coaching staff to find strategies that will be of benefit to the whole team.

PSYCHOLOGY IN BASEBALL

Psychology and **mental strategy** are important in all sports. This is particularly true in baseball, often referred to as the "American pastime." Baseball is also called a "game of brains," in which players enhance their

In baseball, the "game of brains," the whole team needs to be in a game-day mind-set to win.

Sports psychologists can help nervous batters manage their stress to improve their game.

skills by studying their weaknesses and focusing practice on those areas. However, when it is actually game time, players have to shift out of studying their weaknesses and get into the game mind-set. They need to focus only on the game and not on general areas that they need to improve. Sports psychologists work to make sure that team members make this shift.

It is a delicate balance. Players need to be self-aware, but when the game comes, they need to focus on the opposing team and their own teammates. They must have confidence in their own abilities and just play—all the while tracking what other players are doing.

Major League Baseball (MLB) teams generally have sports psychologists on hand in the **dugout**. These psychologists can plan the team's strategy, but they also help players relax, concentrate, and visualize, so that the players themselves can get "in the zone" and use their mind to outplay their opponents. In a game that centers around a ball going 95 miles per hour (153 km/h)—a speed so fast that it can sometimes be hard to see, let alone hit—players must use their minds if they want to win.

CHAPTER 2

THE BASICS OF
Baseball

Baseball is not a complicated game and the rules are not difficult to follow. Although baseball can be played in many places, the setup and equipment is mostly the same, regardless of where the game takes place.

The exact place that baseball began is not entirely known. Some believe it started in France, in as early as the fourteenth century. Others think that the baseball played in the United States today is a version of a game that originated in the United Kingdom.

For a long time, it was thought that baseball was invented in Cooperstown, New York, in the early nineteenth century. However, that theory has been disproved: It is now known that baseball was being played in the United States as early as the late eighteenth century. The game involved a batter standing at the home plate, attempting to hit a ball with a bat. By the 1850s, people were calling baseball the national pastime, and the National Association of Base Ball Players (NABBP) was formed. The rules continued to shift a little as the nineteenth century wore on, but by 1901, the last major change in baseball rules occurred (declaring foul balls to be strikes).

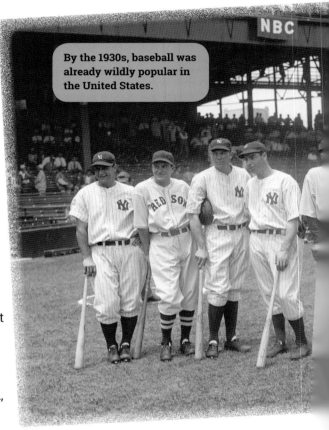

By the 1930s, baseball was already wildly popular in the United States.

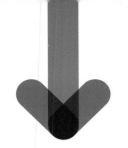

THE LOCATION

Throughout the 1900s and even today, baseball has been played informally in the least likely of locations, using whatever is available. Stickball is a common game for neighborhood children—it roughly follows the rules of baseball, but it is played in the street. Bases are often informally declared. A tree may be used as first base, or a garbage can as home plate. Whoever has a baseball or a bat brings it, teams are made, and the game begins.

Baseball has always been a popular pickup game at events such as community picnics and church outings, too. Sometimes, if the outing is held at a park or schoolyard, there is a baseball diamond present. But at other times, players just put together a makeshift diamond, much like the stickball players in neighborhoods do.

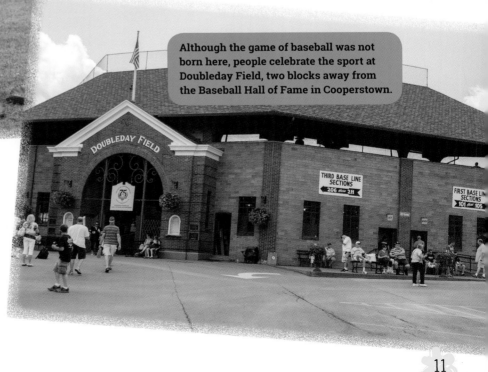

Although the game of baseball was not born here, people celebrate the sport at Doubleday Field, two blocks away from the Baseball Hall of Fame in Cooperstown.

THE DIAMOND

Formally, baseball is played on a diamond. It is a field, but instead of being rectangular like the field football or soccer is played on, it is set up in a diamond shape, with the home plate at the bottom point of the diamond. The rightmost point of the diamond is first base. Second base is at the top of the diamond, and third base is the leftmost point of the diamond. In the middle of the diamond is the pitcher's mound, which is a slightly raised mound of dirt. The first-base line runs from home plate to first base, then extends beyond as a foul line. The third-base line runs between the home plate and third base, and then it extends beyond as a foul line. The base lines are actually invisible, but they follow the white-chalked foul lines that run from home plate to first and third bases, and beyond.

For Major League Baseball, the diamonds are in large, open-air stadiums.

Home plate is where the batter stands as they await the pitch.

The infield is the area inside of the diamond. The area outside of the diamond, but still between the foul lines, is known as the outfield. Just like the infield, the outfield is grassy. The base lines are dirt, and there is some dirt area around the bases. Mostly, the diamond and outfield are covered in grass. The area outside the foul lines is also often grass, and this is known as foul ground.

The bases and home plate are usually white slabs of rubber, as is the pitcher's mound. Around the home plate is a box drawn in white chalk—this is called the batter's box.

On a regulation Major League Baseball diamond, the sides of the diamond are each 90 feet (27 m). So, a player running from home plate to first base must run 90 feet (27 m), a player running from first base to second base must run the same, and so on. The pitcher's plate (on the pitcher's mound) must be 60.5 feet (18 m) away from the back point of home plate.

Baseball can be played anywhere—only a bat and ball are needed.

THE EQUIPMENT

Any game of baseball requires a bat and ball. For informal play, any bat and ball will do, although usually the bat is made from solid wood or hollow aluminum. In professional play, bats must be wooden as aluminum bats are not allowed. The ball is a cork sphere with yarn or string wound tightly around it. The resulting sphere is then covered with stitched leather to get the look of the baseball people know and recognize today.

Bases are also required to play the game. In informal play, bases can be anything—people playing pickup games in the street often use landmarks, such as trees or mailboxes, as bases. However, in formal play, bases are generally either white rubber or canvas bags. Either way, the bases are secured to the ground in formal play, and they are fairly heavy.

Players in the field wear a leather glove on one hand. The gloves help them catch balls more easily. Baseballs move at great speed, and trying to catch one in a bare hand would be painful at best. At worst, a player could end up with a serious injury. The first baseman and the catcher both wear special gloves called mitts. They tend to be better padded and wider than fielder's gloves. Both of these positions require a lot of catching, and the players must protect their hands.

Batters often wear gloves, too, though they are not the special leather gloves designed to help catch a fast-moving ball. Instead, they are thin gloves that give the batter a better grip on the bat. Batters also wear helmets to protect their head and the ear that is facing the pitcher. A Major League Baseball pitcher may pitch a ball at speeds of more than 100 miles per hour (160 km/h). If a batter were hit in the head with such a pitch while not wearing a helmet, a serious head injury could happen. When not batting, players often wear caps that have a wide brim to protect their eyes from the sun.

Catchers are right in the path of speeding pitches, so they wear extra protective gear.

The catcher wears a helmet with a face mask. Remember, the catcher is in the line of fire from that incredibly fast pitch, so they must be protected, too.

In addition to protecting their head and face, the catcher needs to protect the rest of their body. Two important pieces of equipment for catchers are chest protectors and shin guards. These may look somewhat bulky, but they are extremely important for keeping the catcher safe.

Both the catcher and the umpire behind home plate wear face masks to protect them from fast pitches.

CLOTHES AND SHOES

Baseball uniforms consist of tight-fitting pants and a short-sleeved shirt called a jersey. Teams usually have a home and an away uniform. At home, they generally wear white uniforms with their team **logo**, the player's name, and the player's number on them. When they travel for away games, they may switch to a light-gray uniform with the same logo, name, and number on it. Sometimes, teams will wear a colored jersey, either at home or on the road. Some baseball players choose to wear sliding shorts under their pants. These are padded shorts that protect the player's thighs when they are sliding into base.

Baseball players wear cleats. These are shoes with rubber or metal bumps on the bottom to improve the grip when running.

Cleats help baseball players keep their footing when running between the bases or on the field.

THE POSITIONS

There are many positions in baseball, particularly when the team is in the field. When a player's team is up to bat, nearly all players will take a turn. The exception to this rule is in the American League, where there is a designated hitter who bats in place of the pitcher. The team manager sets a batting lineup that players cycle through. When the team is fielding, each player plays a different position out in the field.

The pitcher stands on the pitcher's mound to pitch the ball. They pitch to the catcher, who squats behind the batter. The catcher is also the player who attempts to tag out runners as they approach home plate.

There are three basemen: one each at first, second, and third base. Their primary jobs are to touch the base or tag out players when they catch the ball at their base.

Between the second and third bases is the shortstop. The shortstop is a defensive fielding position. It is believed that more balls are hit to the shortstop than any other fielding position, because most batters are right-handed and tend to hit to the general area between second and third bases.

In the outfield, there are three more fielding positions: left field (out behind the shortstop), center field (roughly behind second base), and right field (in the outfield in between first and second bases).

The outfielders here are close to the infield. For a batter known for powerful hits, the outfielders sometimes move farther out in the field.

YOGI BERRA: LEARN BY WATCHING

It has long been known that mental strategy and psychology play a big role in baseball. Yogi Berra played as a Major League Baseball catcher for 19 seasons. He later went on to be a manager and coach. Berra may be best known for using words incorrectly, but underneath his language mishaps was often thoughtful information.

In one such example, he said, "You can observe a lot by watching." The statement is somewhat obvious, but it is also true and applies very much to baseball psychology. Baseball is a team sport, and players cannot simply assess the strengths of one opponent. They must carefully watch the entire opposing team and look for strengths and weaknesses.

Yogi Berra was known for humorous sayings, but often, there was a lot of baseball wisdom in those statements.

There are numerous players working together on a baseball team. The pitcher tries to strike out each batter. The catcher needs to anticipate the runner coming from third base to home plate and hopefully get them out. The infielders and outfielders have to watch each batter and see where they tend to hit the ball. The basemen need to anticipate whether an infielder or outfielder will be throwing them a fielded ball to get a player out. They must also anticipate whether runners will attempt to steal bases. So much of it is a mind game. The players have to be in top physical shape to hit the ball, pitch, field, and run, but more importantly, they must use their minds to plan how the game will unfold.

CHAPTER 3

COACHING AND TEAM
Strategy

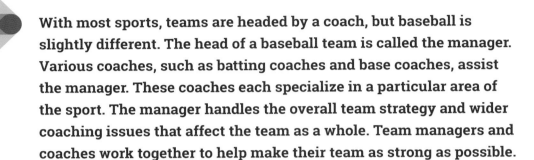

With most sports, teams are headed by a coach, but baseball is slightly different. The head of a baseball team is called the manager. Various coaches, such as batting coaches and base coaches, assist the manager. These coaches each specialize in a particular area of the sport. The manager handles the overall team strategy and wider coaching issues that affect the team as a whole. Team managers and coaches work together to help make their team as strong as possible.

Tommy Lasorda, a former pitcher, famously managed the Dodgers for two decades.

SIMULATING GAME PRESSURE

Learning how to play under pressure is crucial in any sport. It is one thing to play a game for fun, with just fellow teammates around, but it is very different to play in front of a crowd of spectators. There is cheering, there is booing, and there is the unspoken pressure of knowing all eyes are on a given player.

One strategy that managers and coaches use for their teams is to **simulate** playing a real game. Not only does this help players adapt to playing under pressure, it also improves their play psychologically.

Practice is practice, and mentally, players tend to play slightly less than their ability when they know they are not playing in an actual game. Also, newer players who are not used to the pressure of a real game may freeze up during their first games because they are not accustomed to the stress. So, managers and coaches try to simulate the atmosphere of a real game during practice. In this way, they can encourage the best performance from the players and prepare them for the challenges of a real game.

To really get the game-day experience, players may wear their uniforms while they train for a game.

SCRIMMAGING

One way to simulate game pressure is to scrimmage. A scrimmage is a practice session in which teams simulate a game. Baseball coaches from the University of Illinois say they set up scrimmages between members of the baseball squad to simulate the atmosphere of a game.

It is useful for players to do running, hitting, fielding, and pitching **drills**, but these do not feel like a real game. A real game involves all four activities done together—one team is batting and running bases while the other is pitching and fielding. In a scrimmage, the players are able to experience performing multiple baseball activities, rather than just focusing on one at a time. This is important, because, for example, in a catching drill, the players will be focused only on catching a ball thrown by one person in one general direction. Their partner might change up the way he throws the ball—perhaps a curveball one time, a fastball the next. But the throws are still all coming from one person and one general direction.

Scrimmaging allows players to experience many different situations: They are not simply standing in one place, waiting to catch a ball thrown to them.

In a real baseball game, the fielders do not always know quite where a ball will come from or how it will be thrown. A player up to bat will likely hit the ball, and the fielders can reasonably assume the direction and speed it will come from. Those same fielders may also be thrown the ball from another player—perhaps an outfielder throwing the ball to someone playing in the infield. A catching drill will not prepare players for the quick decisions needed in these scenarios, but a scrimmage will.

Although scrimmages simulate the atmosphere of a real game, they are not always as long. While a real baseball game lasts nine innings (assuming one team has won by the end of the ninth), a scrimmage might last only four or five innings. This is enough time to give the players the feel of a game, but it is not so long as to physically exhaust them. There are other practices and games that will require their energy. Still, a good scrimmage can be incredibly useful for getting players in the game mind-set and allowing them to refine their skills.

Pitching is physically exhausting. Often, pitchers are switched out midway through a game, and scrimmages are kept short so as not to exhaust them.

SIGNS AND CALLING THE PITCH

Depending on the team, the manager or the pitching coach may call the pitches. The term "calling pitches" means deciding what type of pitch a pitcher should throw against a particular batter. In Major League Baseball, the catcher often calls the pitches.

Part of the coach's job is to watch the opposing team and identify batters' weaknesses. When they do so, they can use a simple strategy to call the pitch: matching a particular pitch against a batter's weakness. For example, if a coach sees a batter fail to make contact with two curveballs in a row, he can reasonably assume that the batter is not very good at hitting curveballs. He can then communicate to the pitcher to throw a curveball. Since the coach is in the dugout and the pitcher is on the mound, the best way to do this is by using signs.

Pitchers often respond to calls made to them by the catcher or a pitching coach.

SIGNING

Sometimes, coaches use verbal signals to communicate to players, but often, they rely on hand or body signals. These are easier to see from a distance, and they are more challenging for the opposing team to decipher. This last part is important because if the opposing team deciphers the signs, then the element of surprise is lost.

Signs are a very important part of baseball strategy, so players must learn to look for and interpret signs from their coaches. The pitcher has to look for a sign when the coach calls the pitch, and other players must look for signs to **bunt**, **line drive**, or steal a base.

Communication is an important part of baseball psychology. Because it is a team sport, it requires all members of the team to communicate strategy with each other. The best way to do so is by establishing and understanding a system of signing.

When coaches use signs to communicate strategy, players need to be able to read the signs to perform the coach's request.

Regardless of who ends up calling the pitch, signs between players and managers or coaches are the best method of communication for game strategy. When catchers call the pitches, they sign to the pitcher. Together, the catcher, pitcher, and coach can communicate—even while the game is in progress—to refine their strategy against an opposing team.

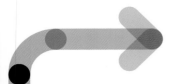

CHAPTER 4

OFFENSIVE Strategies

In baseball, the offensive team is the one that is up to bat. There are two important parts of offensive strategy: hitting strategy and base running strategy.

HITTING STRATEGY

Hitting strategy involves understanding how the pitcher pitches and adjusting the team's strategy accordingly. While waiting for their turn at bat, players can watch a pitcher and assess many things:

- Is the pitcher left- or right-handed?
- Do they throw over the top or use a side arm?
- Do they tend to throw toward one side of the home plate?
- Do they change up the pitches frequently, or do they have a particular type of pitch they tend to use?
- Do they adjust their pitching strategy when there are runners on base versus when there are not?

Ty Cobb, shown here on this commemorative stamp, is one of baseball's legends. He believed that pitchers were usually more afraid of batters than batters were of pitchers.

USA 33

Batters read the game and any signs from their batting coach when they step up to the plate.

Batters can tell a lot about a pitcher just by watching from the dugout. Then, when they are up to bat, they can use this information to devise their strategy, along with any input from the head or batting coach.

To devise their hitting strategy, batters will also assess the game when they come up to bat. If there are runners on base—especially a runner on third, waiting to score—they may employ a different strategy from the one used if the bases are empty. If there is no one on base, the goal is often just to hit the ball hard, so that the batter can make it to at least first base.

Having assessed the pitcher's characteristics and the state of the game at that time, the batter can then decide how best to accomplish his goal: Is this simply to get on base or to bring home runners waiting on second and third?

WHERE TO FOCUS

Finally, before that pitch comes screaming across the plate, batters need to decide where they will focus so they are most likely to make contact with the ball. Some pitchers tend to throw toward the outside of the strike zone, so it makes sense for the batter to focus on the outside of the plate.

Other batters find it more consistent and useful simply to focus straight down the middle. If the ball does indeed come straight down the middle, then they are well set up for a strong hit that will likely result in them making it to base (and potentially bringing someone on third into home, if there are runners on base). Batters could potentially focus on the inside, but since most pitchers try to pitch away from the player, such a strategy is not often terribly useful.

Ball to bat seems like a simple connection, but if a player is not focused, it can be quite challenging.

ALL IN THE MIND

Chipper Jones: Switch-Hitter

One batting strategy that can be incredibly useful is putting a left-handed batter against a right-handed pitcher or vice versa. Unfortunately, many batters do not have the luxury of relying on that strategy. They hit with a particular arm, and they must hit with it, regardless of the pitcher facing them—but not Chipper Jones.

Jones played for 19 years with the Atlanta Braves before retiring in 2012. He is one of the few **switch-hitters** in baseball. In fact, he is one of only two switch-hitters in Major League Baseball history to hit .300 or better from both sides of the plate. This skill has been incredibly useful as he has faced different pitchers. Jones credits his father for forcing him to switch batting arms when he was a boy playing baseball in the yard.

Jones has acknowledged that it takes a lot of effort to be a switch-hitter. However, he says it has paid off for him, because it has given him confidence in facing nearly any pitcher, whether left-handed or right-handed.

One of Chipper Jones' strengths is his unusual ability as a switch-hitter.

Although running the bases seems simple, there is strategy behind it, too.

BASE RUNNING STRATEGY

Hitting the ball is half the battle in baseball. Without a hit, the batter has nowhere to go—unless the pitcher **walks** him. A hit is generally more desirable than a walk, because with a hit, there is the potential to reach farther than just first base.

The other part of offensive strategy, though, is base running. Once a batter hits the ball and is on base, it becomes a matter of how to advance to the next base. The obvious way to advance is to wait for the person at bat to hit the ball and then to run to the next base. This does require some level of strategy, because if the batter hits a fly ball that is likely to be caught by an outfielder, running might not be a wise strategy. If a fly ball is caught and a runner is between bases, the outfielder who caught the fly could throw it to the base the runner came from or the base they were approaching. Either way, the runner could be tagged out. So, while a player on base is likely to run the moment the ball is hit, they need to monitor the ball in the air and make a quick decision about whether to continue or return to base if it looks as if the ball will be caught as a fly.

There are other base running strategies, too. A base runner has only a certain amount of time to make it to the next base. Depending on how well the ball is hit and when it is fielded, it may not be enough time for the runner to get there. One strategy that some base runners use is called hit-and-run, and it involves the runner starting to run toward the next base while the pitcher is throwing the ball, and before the batter has made contact.

The move puts a certain amount of pressure on the batter, who then needs to make contact with the ball in some way. This can be a very effective strategy when a base runner knows that the person up to bat is a strong hitter who is likely to make contact with the ball.

The batter has only a brief moment between hitting the ball and starting his run for first base. He may not even see where the ball is headed when he starts his run down the first-base line.

CHAPTER 5

DEFENSIVE
Strategies

Offense is very important in baseball, since the object of the game is to score as many runs as possible. However, defense is equally important, because without defense, a team will not be able to stop the opposing team from scoring against them. There are two main types of defensive baseball strategies: pitching and fielding.

PITCHING STRATEGIES

In a sense, pitching is the ultimate defense, because if a pitcher has a good game, the other team will not be able to score many runs. If a pitcher can strike out as many batters as possible, there is very little chance for the other team to score.

Pitchers are vital to a good game. If a pitcher has a strong game, it will be difficult for the opposing team to get any hits.

Some pitching strategies are solely based on the pitcher. Pitchers may practice a lot with certain types of pitches, find the ones they are best at, and work to further refine those pitches. Then, when it comes time to pitch to a batter, the pitcher can cycle through several types of pitches to confuse the batter. The pitcher might throw a fastball, then a curveball, then a slider, then another fastball, then a **changeup**. They might start the cycle over again but mix up the order of the pitches, so that the upcoming batters who have been watching will be uncertain of what pitch will be thrown.

Pitchers will try to determine batters' weaknesses when considering what pitch to throw. They always have to outsmart batters to make sure that they do not score runs.

FINDING BATTER WEAKNESS

In determining which pitches to throw, most pitchers will also try to identify a batter's weaknesses and choose their pitches based on these. If a batter struggles with inside curveballs, for example, then the pitcher might decide to pitch that type as one of their pitches.

It is likely that the pitcher would not pitch that type of ball every time to the batter, because half of pitching strategy is to be unpredictable. If the batter who is weak on inside curveballs knows they are coming every time, they can anticipate them and have a better chance of actually hitting one. So, if the pitcher mixes curveballs in with some other pitch types, the batter will be kept off guard and less likely to make contact with the ball.

Keeping the opposition off guard is a psychological strategy used in many sports, and baseball is no exception. If players do not know what to expect, they cannot effectively prepare for what is to come.

TEAM-PITCHING STRATEGIES

One particular pitching strategy affects the entire team in the field, and that is when the pitcher decides to throw pitches that will likely result in a certain type of hit. For example, a pitcher might throw a lot of pitches that will likely produce fly balls. If this is so, then the fielders will want to position themselves to best catch fly balls in the outfield. Or, the pitcher might throw pitches that result in a lot of **grounders**. In this case, the infielders will want to stay close and be on constant alert for grounders, so they can field them and throw them to the basemen as quickly as possible.

The way a pitcher decides to throw the ball affects the other players on his team.

Greg Maddux was not the fastest pitcher in the league, but he may have been the smartest!

ALL IN THE MIND

Greg Maddux: The Smartest Pitcher in the World

Baseball fans and players alike have called Greg Maddux the smartest pitcher in the world. He was a master of strategy during his 23 years of pitching in Major League Baseball. By the numbers, his pitches were not extraordinary—his fastball averaged only 84.3 miles per hour (136 km/h). However, he could outsmart nearly every batter. He was a master at reading a batter from just one swing and adjusting his pitching strategy accordingly.

Such was the case with Luis Gonzalez, who played for the Arizona Diamondbacks. Gonzalez was a good enough hitter to get a fair number of hits off Maddux, and Maddux knew it. So, Maddux turned his weakness into strategy. He told his team manager that if Gonzalez came up to bat, and there were runners in scoring position with an open base, the manager should call for a walk. He knew that if he pitched in the strike zone to Gonzalez, he was likely to hit the ball, and his team would potentially score. It was a safer bet to just walk him.

Maddux's brains on the mound earned him a place in the Baseball Hall of Fame. On the day Maddux was inducted into the Hall of Fame, his pitching coach, Leo Mazzone, said that no other player could compare to Maddux when it came to "thinking the game."

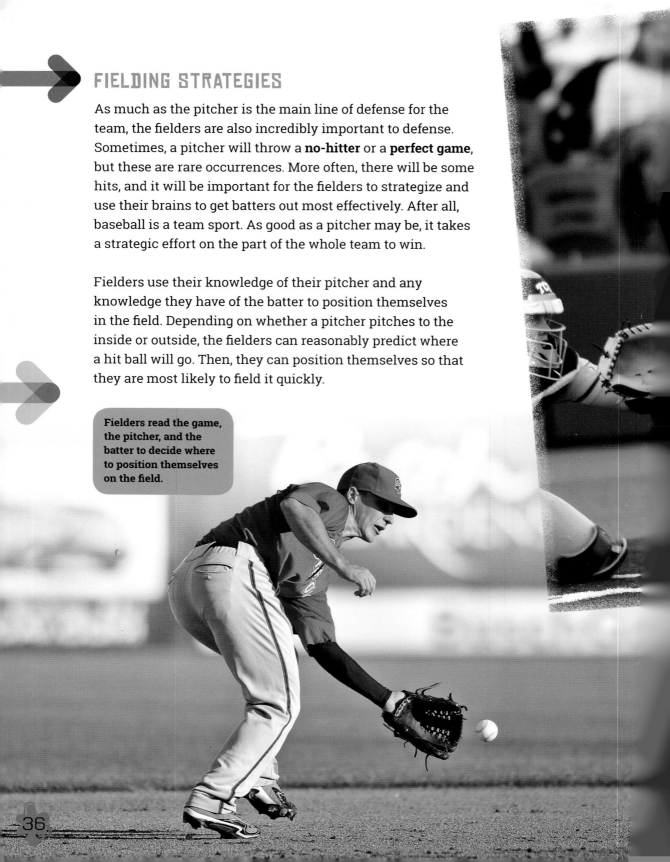

FIELDING STRATEGIES

As much as the pitcher is the main line of defense for the team, the fielders are also incredibly important to defense. Sometimes, a pitcher will throw a **no-hitter** or a **perfect game**, but these are rare occurrences. More often, there will be some hits, and it will be important for the fielders to strategize and use their brains to get batters out most effectively. After all, baseball is a team sport. As good as a pitcher may be, it takes a strategic effort on the part of the whole team to win.

Fielders use their knowledge of their pitcher and any knowledge they have of the batter to position themselves in the field. Depending on whether a pitcher pitches to the inside or outside, the fielders can reasonably predict where a hit ball will go. Then, they can position themselves so that they are most likely to field it quickly.

Fielders read the game, the pitcher, and the batter to decide where to position themselves on the field.

If fielders expect a batter to bunt, they will pull in closer to home plate.

Even if fielders do not know a particular batter well, they can make some simple observations that will help them decide where to position themselves, such as noticing whether the batter is left-handed or right-handed. Sometimes, depending on the game situation, the fielders might have a suspicion that the batter will bunt. For example, if there are no outs, and a batter wants to advance a runner from first to second base (or sometimes from second to third) to better position them to score a run, sometimes the batter will sacrifice the hit and bunt instead. If the fielders see that situation and suspect the batter will bunt, the infielders can pull in and stay close to home plate, so that they can charge the ball and hopefully throw out the base runner.

CHAPTER 6

GAME-DAY

Ready!

> It all comes down to the big game! Game day is what everyone has waited for. All the hours of practice have been building up to this. The practice has not all been physical, either. There have been batting, fielding, throwing, and catching drills, for sure. However, the strongest teams have also been preparing mentally for the game.

When you're game-day ready, you can make game-changing saves like this spectacular catch by right fielder Ryan Ludwick.

38

Players in the dugout try to remain calm and composed as they await their turn at bat.

BIG GAME MENTAL STRATEGIES

Sports psychologists work with baseball players, coaches, and managers to teach them some techniques that will help the team mentally prepare for the big day.

Green Light: Maintain Composure

Composure is crucial in baseball. Players must remain calm and composed at all times to play their best. Ken Ravizza, a sports psychology consultant in Arizona, developed a traffic-signal **analogy** to describe player composure. A green light, which typically means go, means that players are confident, focused on the game, thinking positively, and in control. Green-light players tend to play at the top of their game.

A yellow light, which typically means caution, means players are distracted, anxious, nervous, or frustrated. These players typically are not playing at the top of their game. They may be swinging at bad pitches when up to bat, missing fly balls in the outfield, or pitching poorly while on the mound.

A red light, which typically means stop, means players are in a very negative state. They might be angry, lazy, or uncaring about the game. Either way, they are putting very little effort into the game.

Psychologists can work with baseball players, managers, and coaches to identify when players are going into the yellow or red zones, so that they can make an adjustment and try to shift their composure back into the green zone. The way a player adjusts their composure will vary from person to person, but the first step is to identify when they have slipped from the green zone into the yellow or red.

Visualization for Success

Visualization is a very commonly used technique in all sports psychology, including that of baseball. Sports psychologists teach players how to visualize what they want to accomplish in the game. If they are working on batting, they can visualize themselves making contact with the ball and sending it flying high over the fence for a home run. If they are working on catching, they can visualize the ball landing snugly in their glove. If they are working on pitching, they can visualize the ball sailing neatly over the plate, right in the strike zone, and landing safely in the catcher's glove.

Visualization works for a number of reasons. First, it helps build a skill. If a player visualizes themselves doing something often enough, it eventually becomes a piece of the player's muscle memory—their body learns how to accomplish the skill because it has been "practiced" so many times in the mind.

Second, visualization helps build confidence. If players "see" themselves accomplishing a certain skill enough times, they will begin to believe in themselves more. Confidence is important in any sport, so this is a crucial development that comes from using visualization.

If you can see it, you can do it!

Catchers may visualize themselves tagging runners out before they reach home plate.

There are two types of visualization: internal and external. In internal visualization, the player imagines their body performing the action. It is as if they are actually doing it—only it is just in their mind. In external visualization, the player sees themself performing the action, but it is as if the player is watching a movie of someone else performing the task. Either method of visualization is useful, and neither is preferable over the other.

Using Affirmations

Another way to build confidence is by using positive affirmations. Psychologists often recommend that players use daily affirmations. The idea is that, if a person hears something often enough, they really will start to believe it. So, for example, a pitcher might say every day, "I am the strongest pitcher in the league. My pitches consistently fall into the strike zone, and I strike out most batters who come up to the plate."

Sports psychologists say affirmations can be done either verbally (as in speaking out loud) or in writing, by keeping an affirmation journal or writing a letter of affirmation to oneself. Some athletes find it useful to recite affirmations in a mirror, so they can see themselves while doing it. Others do it during specific everyday routines, such as taking a shower or getting ready for bed. They find that if they link the affirmations to a routine, they will actually remember to do them. With athletes who choose written affirmations, some write the affirmations once and then reread them frequently. Others find the act of repeatedly writing the positive statements (ideally, at least once a day) useful. Either way, it is important that the player revisit these affirmations as often as possible.

Focus, Focus, Focus

Sports psychologists also emphasize the importance of building focus in baseball. They encourage players to focus on what they can control, such as their own performance. Baseball is a team sport, so there are a lot of people involved and many things a player cannot control.

A runner bearing down on the home plate needs to focus on reaching the plate, even when it looks as though a catcher may be in the way.

A strong psychological game makes for a winning team!

So, psychologists recommend that players focus on their own attitude and their own strategy when facing off against another player.

Psychologists also recommend that baseball players focus on the present. While there is value in considering what a player's weak spot was in another game or in practice, it is useful to do that long before the game or after the game. It is not useful to do that right before a game or, worse yet, during a game. That will only distract the player and possibly put them in a negative mental space. During and right before the game, players should focus only on the game at hand.

TY COBB: TURNING WEAKNESS INTO STRENGTH

Ty Cobb was a good hitter but not a terrific base runner. Winning a game of baseball requires running the bases to score, so Cobb rightfully saw an area that it would benefit him to improve. He spent hours by himself, practicing running and sliding into bases, until he knew he had improved from being an average base runner to a good one. At the same time, he kept his mind focused on what he felt was the overall strategy of baseball.

Cobb knew that the way to be an outstanding baseball player was to practice until his weakness was a strength. He also knew that it was important to keep in mind the overall strategies of assessing the situation every time he was at bat or on base. Then, he used his knowledge of that situation to determine whether it was a time to bunt, a time to steal, or a time to punch through an opening in the opposition's defense.

In this sense, baseball is not simply a game of one strategy. It is a game of keeping in mind many strategies and using one's mind to evaluate the best one to use at any given time. Ty Cobb was a master of that.

Part of Ty Cobb's (left) strength as a player was his willingness to see his weaknesses and work on them.

THE ART AND SCIENCE OF THE GAME

In the end, baseball has features of both art and science. There is science in the mechanics of it—physics in the way the batter swings the bat and connects it with the ball, and in the way the ball arcs through the sky to the waiting fielders.

The strategy—the other important part—is both art and science in one. Strategy requires scientific analysis of how the ball moves and how a particular player plays, and it also requires the art of connecting that information and forming an offensive or defensive strategy. Using psychology to better one's game takes the best of both science and art and pulls it together into strategy.

Spring training is a great time to see baseball players gearing up for a winning season.

GLOSSARY

analogy a comparison between two things, used to explain a concept

athleticism strength, fitness, and agility in an athlete

bunt to gently tap a ball with the bat, rather than swinging and trying to hit it as hard as possible

changeup a slow pitch thrown with the same motion as a fast pitch, designed to trick the batter

coordination the ability to use different body parts together at the same time

drills repeated practice exercises designed to work on a particular skill

dugout a seating shelter at the side of a baseball diamond where teams sit during the game

goal setting setting small, manageable goals to achieve an overall greater goal

grounders balls that, when hit, stay very close to the ground or roll along the ground

line drive a ball that, when hit, stays low and parallel to the ground

logo an identifying symbol

mental state a state of mind

mental strategy plans to help someone meet a goal

neuroscience science dealing with the function of the brain and nervous system

no-hitter a game in which no batters get a hit off the pitcher

perception the ability to become aware of something through the senses

perfect game a game in which no batters reach first base by any means—hits, walks, or errors

psychology the study of the mind and its functions

simulate to imitate the appearance of something else

switch-hitters batters who can hit from either side of the home plate (left- or right-handed)

visualization forming a mental image of an action or object

walks when a batter does not swing at four pitches that are all outside the strike zone, they are allowed to walk to base, and any players on base already are allowed to walk to the next base

FOR MORE INFORMATION

BOOKS

Adamson, Thomas K. *The Technology of Baseball.* North Mankato, MN: Capstone Press, 2013.

Graubart, Norman D. *The Science of Baseball.* New York, NY: PowerKids Press, 2016.

Holub, Joan. *Who Was Babe Ruth?* New York, NY: Grosset & Dunlap, 2012.

WEBSITES

Find out more about sports and fitness at:
www.brainpop.com/health/sportsandfitness

Learn more about baseball at:
www.ducksters.com/sports/baseball.php

Read up on Major League Baseball at:
mlb.com/mlb/kids/index.jsp

Sports Illustrated Kids has a lot of information on baseball at:
www.sikids.com

Publisher's note to educators and parents: Our editors have carefully reviewed these websites to ensure that they are suitable for students. Many websites change frequently, however, and we cannot guarantee that a site's future contents will continue to meet our high standards of quality and educational value. Be advised that students should be closely supervised whenever they access the Internet.

INDEX